REFRESHING MANDALA COLORING BOOK FOR ADULTS

[Document subtitle]

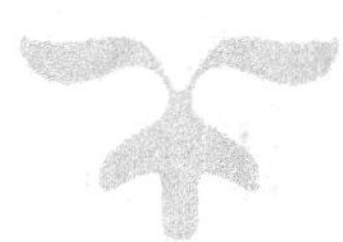

NOVEMBER 22, 2018
AUTHOR – SADDAM NA
New Delhi

Krish Amin (c) 2015

ing pages

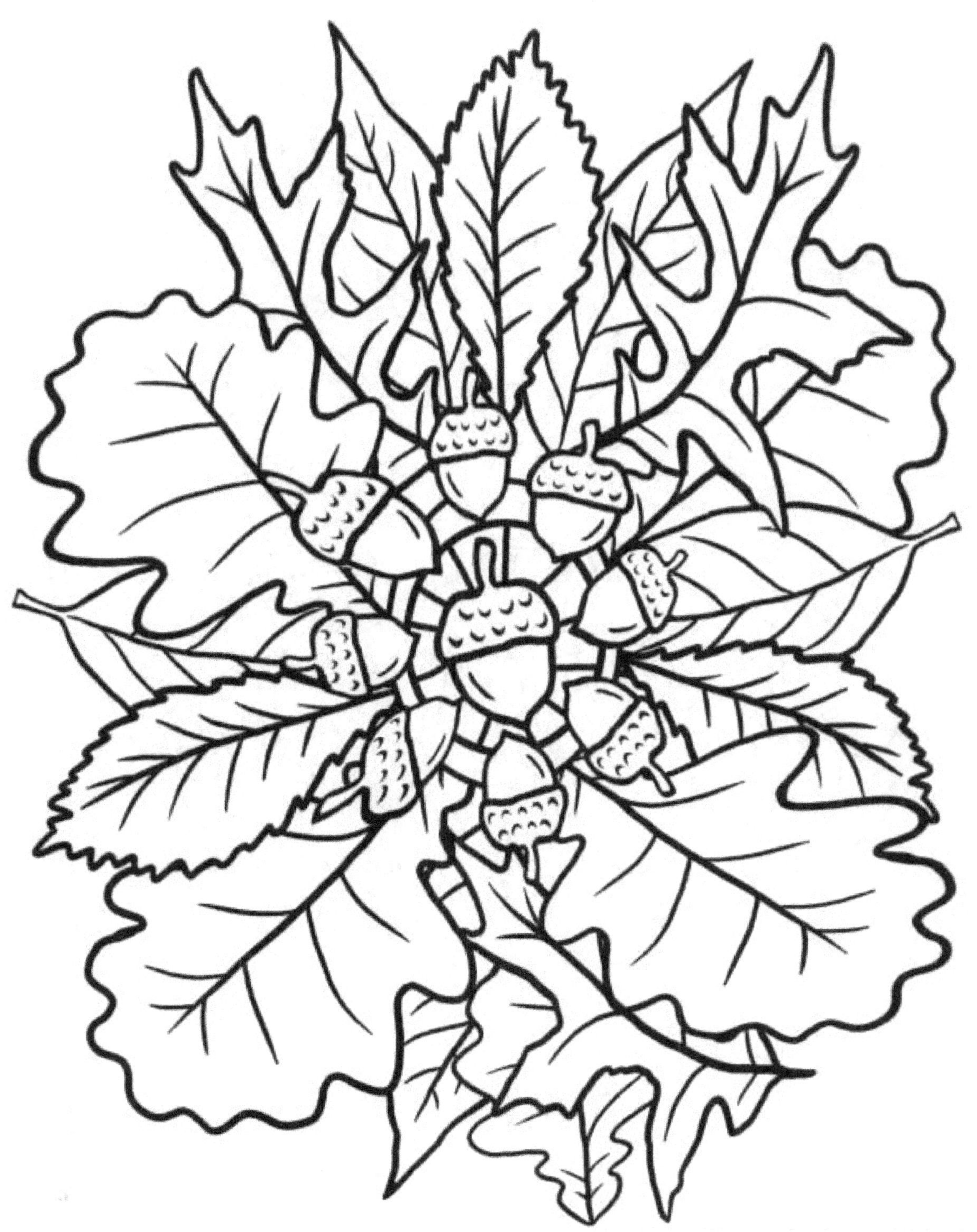

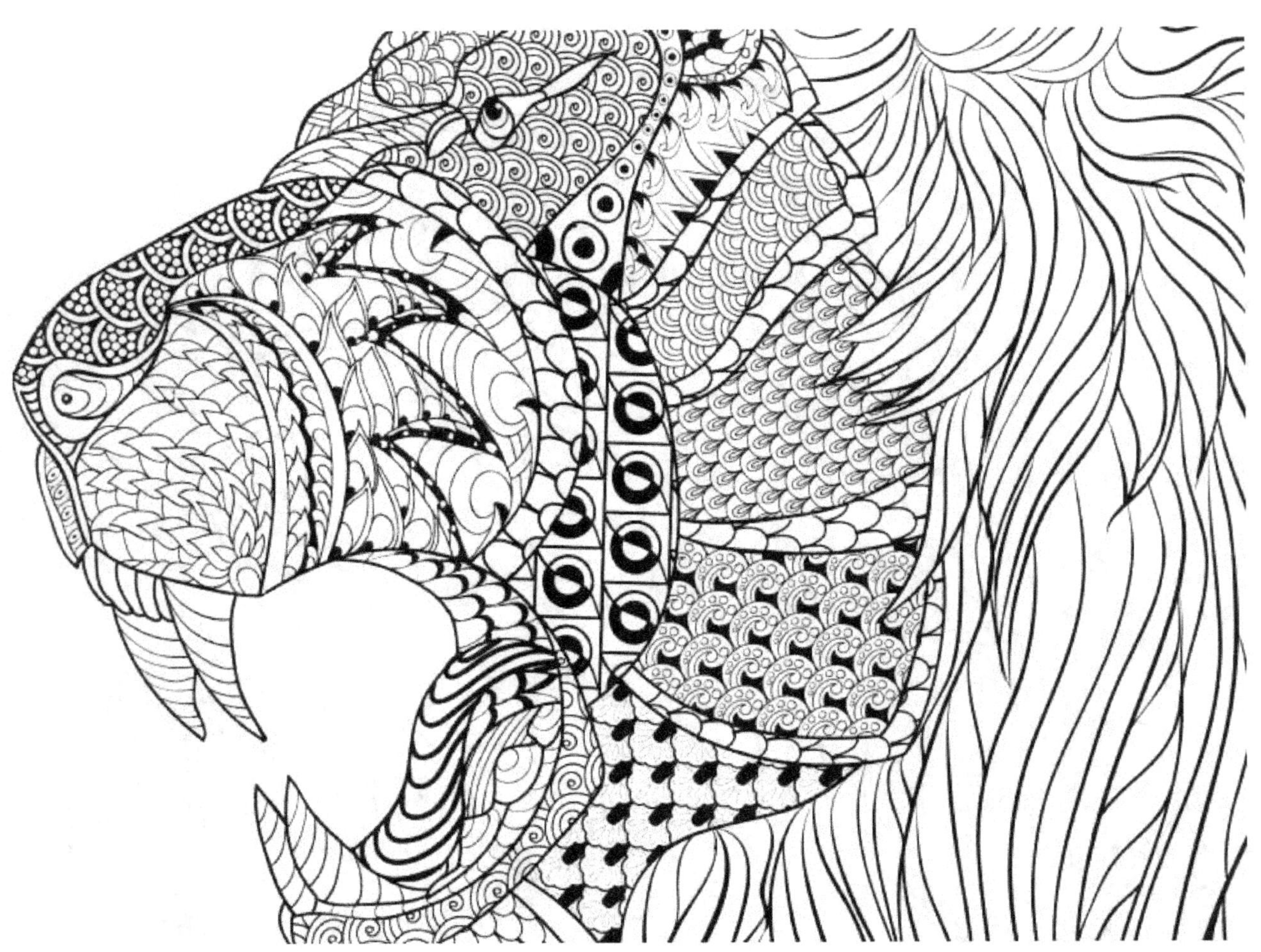

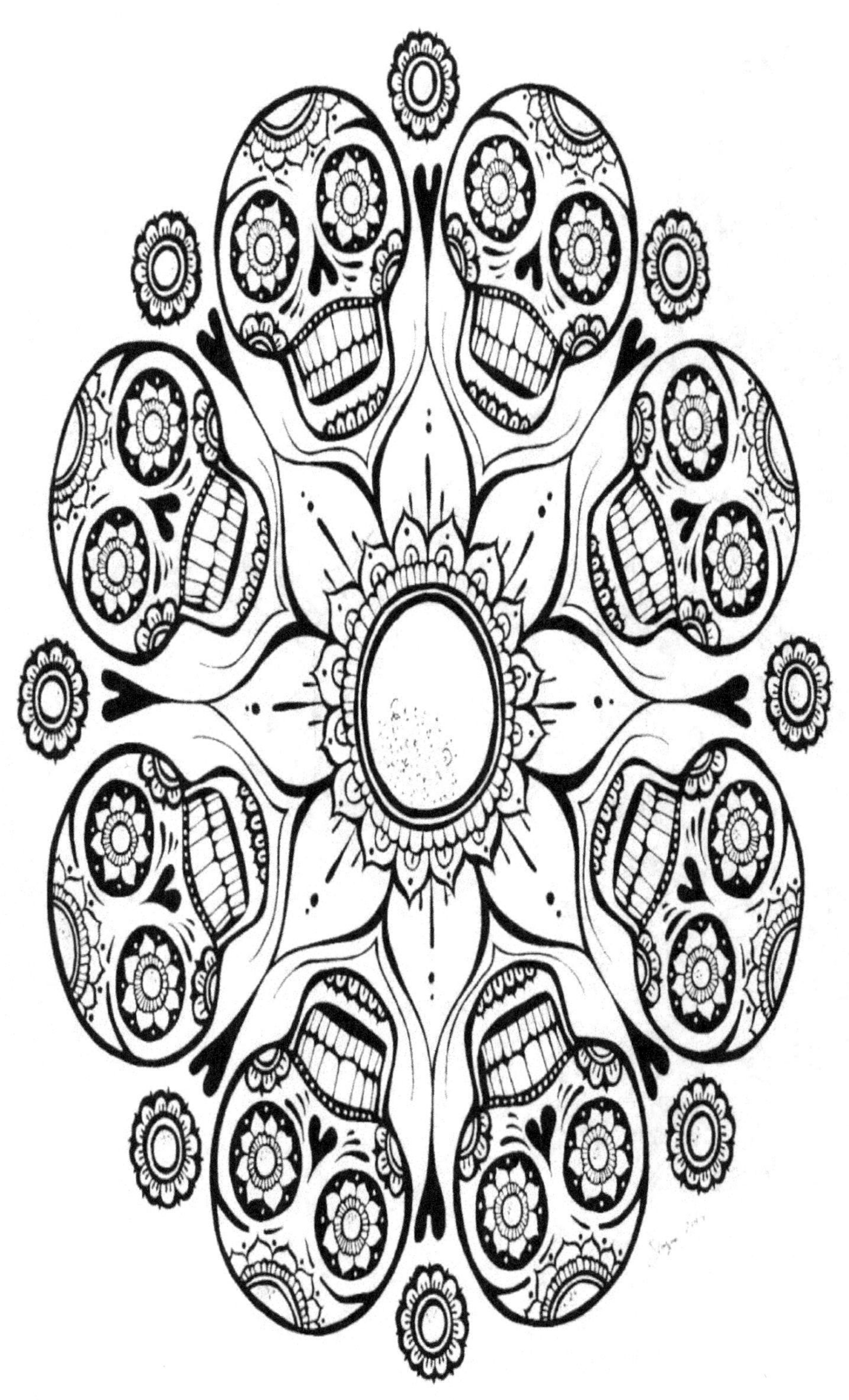

MOODY

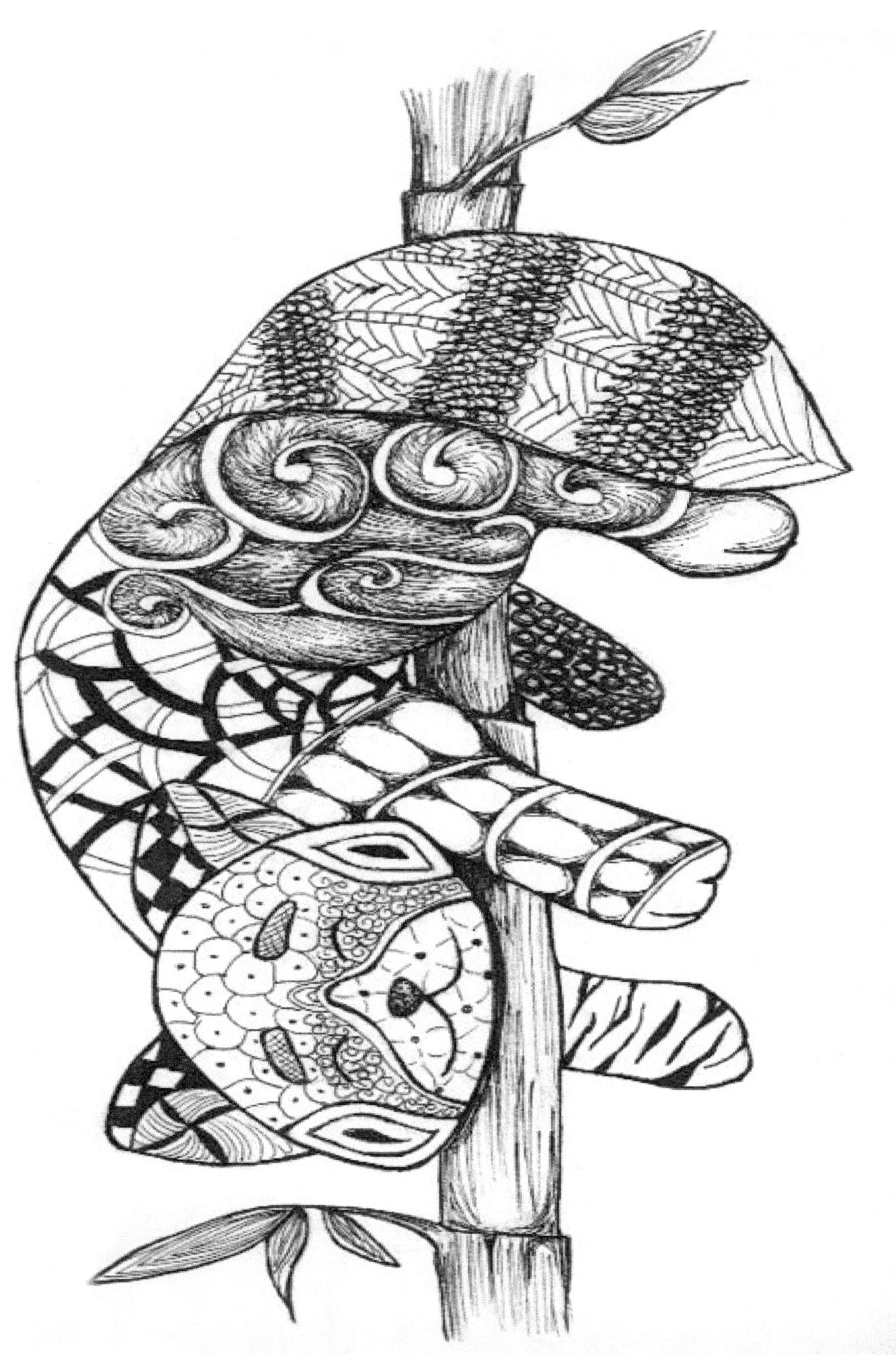

PiNG
5

Breathe

paint the world
SUPER
COLORING

Copyright Julie Kukreja All Rights Reserved

ColorPagesforMom.com

www.coloring-pages.info

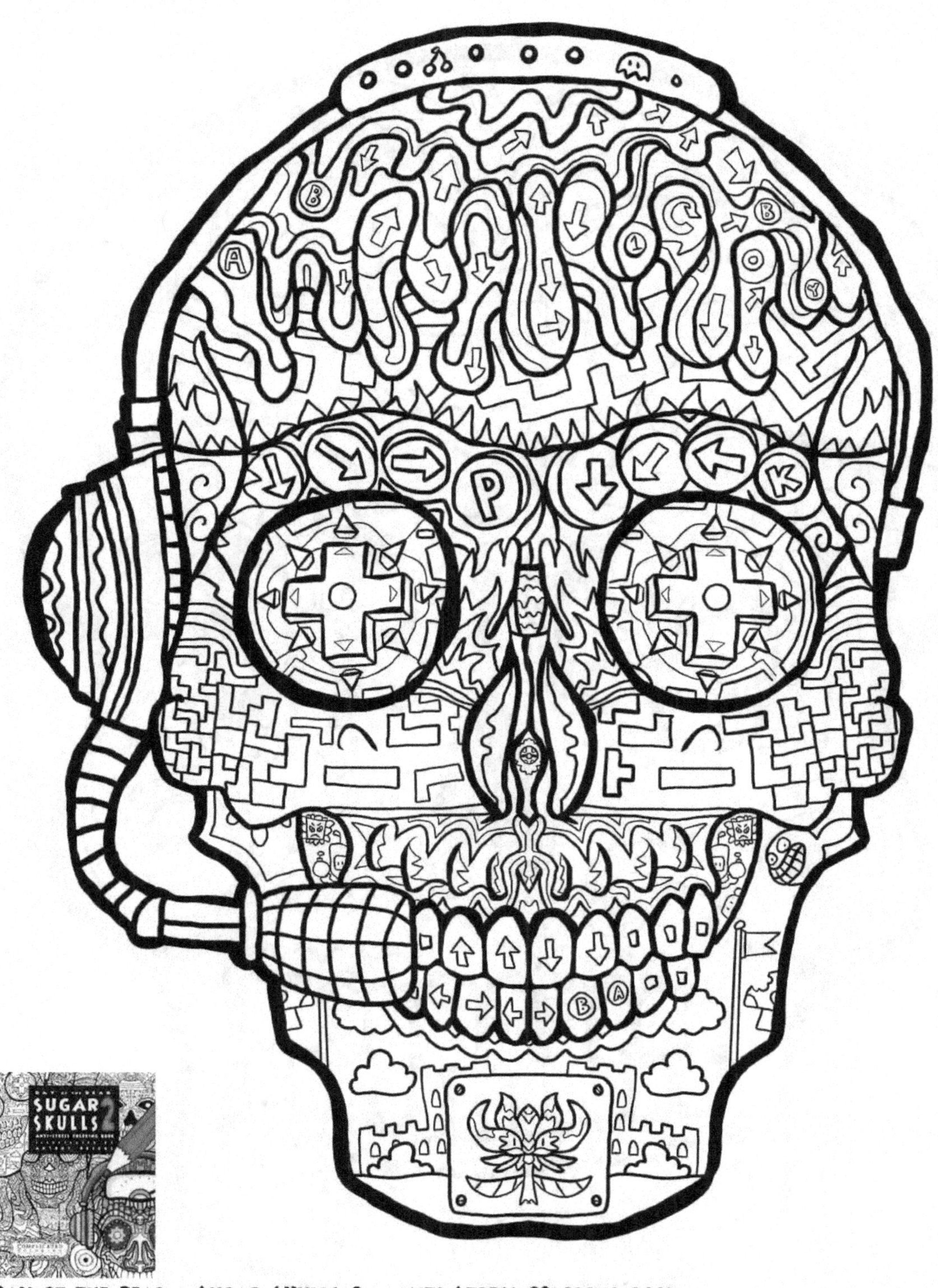

DAY OF THE DEAD - SUGAR SKULLS 2 - ANTI STRESS COLORING BOOK
BY COMPLICATED COLORING - OUT NOW ON AMAZON - WWW.COMPLICATEDCOLORING.COM

GRYFFINDOR

PESCNO.BLOGSPOT.COM

COOL2BKIDS.COM

www.coloring-pages.info